Everyday Sacred

Everyday Sacred

Meditations and Paintings
to Inspire Reflection and Prayer

Clarence Heller
Artwork by the author

Marjoejess Imprints

Designed by Meadowlark Publishing Services.
Subjects: Spiritual Poetry and Art
Christian Meditations
Ignatian Prayer
ISBN 978-1-4507-2725-9
Manufactured in the United States of America.
Published 2010

Marjoejess Imprints™
www.clarenceheller.com

Dedicated to Marilyn, Joe, and Jessica
with special thanks …

to Marian Cowan, C.S.J., who encouraged
me to paint and to discern,

to the many friends who offered affirmation
and encouragement regarding my prayers,
poems, and reflections,

and to Pat Tovo, without whom
this book would still be only a vision.

Contents

"When you want what you have,
  and when you love who you are,
  you will desire to give yourself away …"

Introduction

Love surprised me.

As I was riding home in the backseat of my parents' car with my girlfriend after a warm summer day at the lake, tears welled in my eyes. It was my first experience of true happiness, and my first taste of joy. It was August 1972, and we had been dating for three months. I was sixteen years old. As I reflect back to that time, I realize that the first love poems I wrote, about twelve in all, came during our first year of dating. I would type them on colored paper and in return she would give me one of the ribbons that tied her hair. The poems stopped coming, but the love affair kept growing. Today, Marilyn and I continue to celebrate our life together.

I needed to be loved. As a teenager then and for much of my life afterward, I operated out of a deeply rooted sense of insecurity and inadequacy. I know what it is to be driven to prove yourself even though you are the only one keeping track. I know what it is to be competitive and ambitious, to sacrifice love, family, and relationship with God for the subconscious objective that someday, somehow you will prove you are good enough. Even when I tried to let go of ambition, it found ways to creep back in, and before I realized it I was again working endless hours to achieve more, to be the best I could be. And it was never enough. It never could be enough.

I recall working in a warehouse at a retail store during my high school years. When I started the job, I was one of three people staffing the warehouse on Saturdays. Within a year, I was the only staff person, yet the work load remained the same. In college, I received a 99 percent test score in differential equations when a classmate earned 100 percent. I vowed that "failure" would never be repeated. And I recall with sadness that a few years after completing my masters in business administration while working full time, I noticed a picture of a three-year-old girl hanging in our hallway. I wondered why a photograph of my niece would be in such a prominent place in my home—then realized it was one taken of my daughter while I was busy pursuing that masters degree.

Despite my frequent absence from their lives, my family continued to love me. God continued to love me, and through love comes healing. In my early forties, God began to seduce me, and I surrendered to the invitation. My first tiny yes led to another. The next experience of love led to wanting even more and to being more open and free to receive it and respond. God is such a great lover. Thank you, God.

At the age of forty-five, I wanted to change my life, and I decided to retire and study theology. I had always been Roman Catholic, learning from the School Sisters of Notre Dame in elementary school and the Brothers of Mary in high school. I attended church most Sundays, but it meant very little. Honestly, I did not know it could mean more than it did then.

During my first year at Aquinas Institute of Theology, I began receiving the counsel of a spiritual director (thank you, Madeleine and Marian) and participated in *The Spiritual Exercises of Ignatius Loyola* (the Nineteenth Annotation). My life changed profoundly. I came to have a personal relationship with Jesus, and my healing took a leap forward. It was as though I had embarked upon a very important journey home, one long overdue.

One prayer technique we employ in *The Exercises* invites God to use our memory and imagination to help us enter into one of the stories in the Gospels, in a very personal way. One day I prayed with the post-resurrection scene in which Peter and his companions fish while Jesus stands, unrecognized, on the beach (John 21:1–14). In the prayer, I took on the role of Peter. We followed Jesus' instructions to cast the net on the other side of the boat, and it soon overflowed with fish. Immediately I realized the man giving instruction was Jesus, jumped in, and swam ashore. As we

collected the great catch ("153 large fish") I noticed something peculiar about these particular fish. In my prayer, the fish were indeed large, each weighing perhaps twenty-five pounds, and they were brilliantly colored in a range of hues. But their most spectacular feature was that they smiled broadly, very happily.

"What should I do with these fish?" I asked Jesus.

He replied, "Throw them back so that they can tell the others."

"Telling the others" is what this book is about. It is what my life is about, and it is what I understand Jesus' mission to be about—helping others come to know that they are deeply and unconditionally loved.

Four years after my colorful prayer, I graduated with a masters in pastoral studies (emphasis in adult Christian formation) and a certificate in spiritual direction. Both of these paved my way to assist adults in entering more deeply into a relationship with God.

On July 24, 2003, during prayer—now two years after I retired—my urge to write poetry returned. Love surprised me again. I had spent the day walking the streets of Wellston, a municipality at the edge of the St. Louis city limits, a neighborhood of those less privileged. I had been going door to door informing residents how they could arrange to have their children transferred for free to a higher-quality school system. Again, the seduction continued with a small opening that led to more. This is the poem I wrote:

Wellston

Sore knuckles, sweaty brow,
Trying to love, but not sure how,
But it isn't how or when or where,
It is in the trying that people know I care.

Since then, more than three hundred meditations (poems and reflections) and a hundred paintings have come to me. But I am not so much an author or artist as I am a pray-er. Before beginning each painting I surrender all of myself to God (body, mind, spirit, emotions, will, intellect, imagination, subconscious, and whatever else of me there is) and ask God to say to me whatever God wishes through the painting. I ask to be able to tell God what is deep inside myself through the painting. I use my nondominant hand to finger paint, with the hope of letting go even further any perceived control I may have. And I lose myself. It is a process of nonthinking, nonverbal, emotional, authentic expression in which the colors choose themselves and I am often surprised at what appears on the paper. It is a being and doing with God.

The process of writing also occurs in the context of prayer, most often during a block of time I have intentionally set aside to pray. When I am moved to write, it always starts with a word or two that opens the door to a sacred space, and then I pick up my pen and write in my notebook. It is not a process of composing and, as with the painting, I am frequently surprised by what appears on the page. When I finish, I am often moved to tears; I might even laugh out loud. The best way I can describe the process of this holy writing is that it is like romantic kissing: I lose track of where I stop and where the Other begins. It is an interactive process. It is an act of welcoming and surrendering, giving and receiving.

Great blessings in my life have been Sr. Mary Funge of the Society of Helpers and what she has given me. Mary brought a program called Week of Guided Prayer—A Retreat in Everyday Life to St. Louis in 1995, and in 2005, with her eightieth birthday approaching, she needed someone to take over running it. She asked me to, and I jumped at the opportunity. Since that time, I have led more than thirty of these retreats, serving more than five hundred retreatants. It is a graced ministry. Thank you, God, again. During many of the retreats, I am afforded time to be with God, write down what God offers, and describe what I offer to God. Slowly at first, I began to share with other spiritual directors and retreatants some of these meditations for their own use during prayer times if they wished.

The affirmation and encouragement I received were overwhelming. Many people approached me and expressed how deeply the meditations touched them. They shared the writings with friends and used them when leading groups in prayer. I discovered that these small works were finding their way into Bibles and onto refrigerators for daily reflection and inspiration. I was told time and again that my writings were different from other spiritual poems and prayers because readers deeply resonated with the words and messages; these reflected what they knew and how they felt but could not express.

The paintings and writings are repeated blessings. The most precious fruits of my conversion, however, are the relationships in my life, all of which have become more loving and authentic: relationships with my wife, children, parents, friends, self, and God. I recall that one day about six months after I started at Aquinas Institute, my son said out of the blue, "You know, Dad, you're not as crabby as you used to be." For the past several years, each time my parents and I meet, we hug and say "I love you," something we did not even know we longed for ten years ago. My relationship with Marilyn has blossomed into a rich, mature romance much more profound than I imagined anyone could experience. She has helped me discover that what love wants most for the other is freedom. Most importantly, now I know in my head and heart that I am loved for who I am, as I am, and this awareness opens me to love everything and everyone more fully, freely, and authentically.

As part of the process of navigating toward publishing this book, a collaborator on this project (thank you, Pat) encouraged me to create an intention board in the form of a collage, and I did. As with painting, I approached this as a form of prayer, and I was very pleased with the result. It was full of joy, abundance, and freedom, and the strongest theme to emerge was connecting. One part of it says "It's your gift: connecting new." And I believe this is true. I have a passion for helping others "connect new": to bring awareness to what they already understand deep down but have lost or forgotten, and use this awareness to reconnect with each other, with God, and with their authentic selves. The Week and Month of Guided Prayer retreats do exactly this, and to the extent that this book does as well, it is an extension of my living in consonance with my purpose in life.

A Walk Through the Chapters

As a spiritual director, I am likely to ask a retreatant or directee, "How do you experience God?" My question is not "*Do* you experience God" but "*how?*" The fact is that God is with us, even though we may not recognize a particular experience as God or as being of God. The response to this question is often something like "Well, I don't know if this counts, but I most easily experience God in nature, or when I am holding my grandchild. Actually when I think about it, I experience God more often in everyday life than when I am at church." I usually say that it is not for me to decide whether such an experience counts, but that I would like to hear more about it. I jump for joy inside myself and hope that I can lead the person deeper into such experiences so they can believe them, claim them, welcome them, and recognize them more easily. Yes, what a privilege it is to be a spiritual director.

This book carries the same hope—that I will help others come to know God more deeply and to claim lives filled with sacredness.

Our first chapter, Nature, focuses on experiencing God through this most frequent and profound medium for revelation. Whether it is the beauty of a sunset, the power of a waterfall, the delicacy of a frost flower, or the "silence" of a forest, God not only speaks through nature; we are able to hear.

We then turn our attention to Home. A friend once described home as the place where we feel safe. While this is true for many people, a sense of safety at home is but a distant dream for many others. Yet God is there with us, in good times and in bad. Rejoicing, comforting, and suffering with us even when we may not experience God's presence. Let us grope together to find God with us, and when we long for God's compassion, let us be compassion for each other (in God).

We move on to Family. As human beings, we are created for relationship: with other people, with God, and with ourselves. Our first relationships, and the ones that may have the longest-lasting impact in our lives, are the ones we experience in the context of family. And God is there with us.

As a Christian, I believe that the most perfect, complete revelation of God was Jesus of Nazareth. Fully human and fully divine. A man who was born, lived, suffered, played, loved, died, and rose from the dead. As a Christian, I believe that the flesh is important, that the physical dimension of our existence is important. The flesh

is not something to be overcome or a pit stop on the way to eternal life, but a means of experiencing and expressing God in the world. Yes, we are spiritual beings, but enfleshed spiritual beings. The Word became flesh that we may come to know God more fully. We became flesh for the same reason and so God could be in relationship with us. So often, we dismiss or overlook the humanness, the beautiful humanness of Jesus—the one like us in all things but sin. Yet this excludes the possibility of a relationship with Jesus that can be very powerful, an aspect of Him that can lead to deep love relationship, friendship, and mutuality. Thus, the chapter entitled Jesus.

And because the flesh is important, Jesus also offers his flesh to us through the Eucharist, and with our flesh we become united with Christ and with each other in Christ. In the chapter called Holy Communion, I invite you to explore how we may experience holy communion both Sacramentally with a capital S and in the context of our families and everyday relationships. Holiness and our encounters with God have no boundaries—if we are open. Our longing for union with each other and, if we are aware, with God, is primordial, from our first moment in the world to our last.

Depending upon your experience with church or "The Church," you may find the inclusion of the chapter called Church quite natural or completely inappropriate. That is precisely my point. Sometimes, some of us do encounter the Divine in the context of church, and is it not right to honor that as well? Sometimes, for some of us, our interaction with church informs the rest of our

Nature

"And when all memory of me has passed away,
still I will know,
still I will know,
that I always was,
and I always will be,
a part of God."

Heaven

I woke up in heaven today …
I could hear the angels singing praises to God
through the voices of the birds.
I could see the majesty of life energy
manifested through budding flowers and leaves—
white, green, yellow, blue, mauve.
I could witness freedom as birds soared and swooped,
as butterflies fluttered along,
and through my choice whether to be attentive.
I was blinded by the beatific vision of the sun,
and the sky,
and a young child's smile.
I woke up in heaven today,
and wondered, "What do people do in heaven?"
and I suppose the answer may be
enjoy life,
share love,
participate in beauty,
and praise God in the process.

I Accept

I can't create a tree,
make cells out of nothing,
or make them grow and multiply and blossom.
I can't imagine an insect I've never seen,
or a sound I've never heard,
or what it might be like beyond the limitlessness of space.
But I can help someone feel loved,
and that is all God has called me to do.
Yes, I accept that I am not God,
that I cannot do the things only God can do,
but I also accept that I am of God and in God
and that, in communion with God,
I am invited to love the world around me.
In deep gratitude, I accept.

Earth Tones

Always green trees welcome
gentle white snowflakes.
Yellowed grass hibernates.
Fertile earth brown waits.
How can anyone say
we are not already in heaven?

There is a peculiar story in Mark's Gospel (8:22–26) of Jesus healing a blind man. After a first attempt, the man said, "I can see people, but they look like trees, walking.' Then Jesus laid hands on his eyes again ... and he saw everything clearly." This made me wonder if that man could in fact see so well as to appreciate our connectedness with nature but, not appreciating this gift, wished to see only in the conventional sense.

Walking Trees

To see people as walking trees
is to see more clearly than most.
Oh, to be aware that my flesh
is but soil fleetingly transformed,
and that my blood is water borrowed
from the rivers and the seas.
Oh, that I may be as faithful as a tree,
as holy as a rock,
as selfless as a flower.
I gladly return the life
you have given me, Mother Earth ...
    that life may carry on,
    that others may live,
    that we may be reunited.

And when all memory of me has passed away,
still I will know,
still I will know,
that I always was,
and I always will be,
a part of God.

Unquenchable Longing

As a tree searches and strives for deeper connection with God
through its roots to the earth
and its branches to the sky,
let your love search my heart,
my soul,
my body,
and let me strive with you
so that we may find each other
inseparably interwoven.

Autumn en Joy

Amber-orange, green and browning
All dressed up for glorious downing
Welcoming the inevitable molting
New life begins without so much jolting
As we often impose, fearful resistance
It is Love's way to invite with persistence
To surrender

Is There Any Sound?

If the wind blows but has contact with nothing,
is there any sound?
Isn't the purpose of leaves to be the vehicle for the wind to speak
and the energy of the sun to be transformed into life?
Aren't people the same, our purpose to be a means for God
to express boundless love and energy in a form that is tangible?
We are strings that create music as God's energy
stimulates us into motion.
A chorus of love: leaves, birds singing, dogs barking,
people talking, footsteps,
and my heart beating, pounding, yearning to be in harmony
with what you are creating.
I feel so powerless and yet
the most powerful tool I have to cooperate with you is my desire,
my deep desire,
which originates in you.
Thank you feels inadequate,
and that's not really what you long for,
instead, you hope that I will accept your invitation
to come out and play in this garden of paradise,
to enter into your yearning, joy, suffering,
life, and love.

During prayer in the park. Ever so gently, a feeling comes over me that I am being embraced by the nearby tree, and that I am deeply connected with Mr. Earth, who has become incarnate below the grass near me.

For an Older Audience

Forty-five years later and I'm still hoping
to be one of the Do-Bees (Do-Be).
You know, from Romper Room.
To be affirmed, to be accepted,
to feel loved and interconnected with others.
Yes, that's still what I long for.

I still desire to follow the rules, but now
the rules are different …
to love, to be loved, to be aware,
to be vulnerable,
to search out and strengthen connectedness,
to work against isolation in all its forms.
And whatever I do, to foster that those actions
may flow out of my state of being,
to do everything out of love, freedom, and truth,
(at least that is my hope)
to embrace the fact that I am never alone
because Jesus is with me always.

So sometimes I just sit in the sun,
pay attention to how good it feels on my skin,
and I thank God for that feeling.
I close my eyes and listen for the sounds of life …
people walking, talking, leaves rustling, myself breathing,
and I thank God for the gift of hearing.
I then open my eyes and try to see what has always been there
but I have not yet noticed
(it is always so much),
and I thank God for the gift of eyesight.
Sometimes that is my doing,
to stop and let God love me,
and to say thank you,
thank you,
thank you.

My wife and I visited Big Basin Redwoods State Park, south of San Francisco. Some of the trees there are about 2,000 years old, 330 feet tall, and 18 feet in diameter. It was a spiritual experience.

The Forest

I hugged an enormous tree,
a really enormous tree,
more enormous than you would think,
and I'm not sure it noticed
little me …
begging attention like a toddler clinging to her mother's leg,
and was it really the point that the tree would notice …
my touch,
my breath,
my presence?

My presence there was fleeting,
a blink in the life of that tree
as old as Jesus.

So small,
so very transitory,
so insignificant and powerless,
I love you tree, I do.
Thank you for putting me in my place.

Yes, it was that place,
the forest,
where God seeped out,
not in the enormous tree,
not just there,
not just in the earth,
not just in the smells of dry wood and dust
and the occasional pine needle.
No, God was in the fabric.
God was the fabric of the forest.
Timeless energy,
in the living,
and in the dying and decay,
in the air and the earth,
ineffable yet present,
unchangeable in the midst of the
unceasing life cycle of the forest,
and I was there too.

Did you feel me, God?
Did you notice me there, if only for a moment?
And does it change anything if You did?

Waving

Cottonwood leaves are waving …
    hello
    welcome
    peace
    gentleness
    acceptance
    life
    a sense of being
    all is well
    do you see us?
    do you notice us?
    can you hear us?
    you are always welcome here.

And while you appreciate us
we appreciate you …
    beauty
    joy
    energy
    a sense of being
    all is well

Grateful for each other.
Grateful for all.

Autumn Goodness

Today, the Immense Goodness spewed from the depths
like juice from a fully ripe piece of fruit
on the tip of God's tongue
so close I can touch it
see it, smell it
experience its transition
as another leaf falls and
others deepen their hue before my eyes
if dying can be so beautiful
then let me die also
perfect imperfection of individuality
I too yearn to be an instrument of love
past and future converge in the present
never stopping, but pausing to notice
that God is here among us

Radiance

Like an autumn leaf,
A soul's inner beauty shines
In sweet surrender.

Tickled

If God sneezed,
the earth's rotation would sputter,
endangered species would become extinct,
the omniscience of complete attentiveness would be interrupted.
Yet we try to tickle God's nose
and blow dust with innocent self-absorption
and fear of becoming ONE.
"Leave me alone," we say.
"Your love overwhelms me.
I want to hide (but just for awhile)."
Parent and child teasing,
playfulness of love.
You love me so much sometimes it hurts.
I am forced to look away from the sun,
yet still feel the warmth and see its light.
I want you to tickle me (I love the attention),
but not so much that I might pee a little.

Miracles

If we didn't see the miracle, does that mean it didn't happen?
If something occurs so often that we fail to even notice,
can it not still be miraculous?
We say what a miracle life is when we witness a birth,
but the miracle of life occurs each time we breathe,
each time there is thought,
each time a heart beats,
each time love brings someone to tears,
each time a tiny cut heals
or a broken bone mends,
each time a bird flies
or a spring peeper rejoices so loudly,
and each time a firefly lights.
Yes, life is the miracle love brings forth
each moment, in innumerable ways.
Thank you, oh loving God, for the miracle of this day.
Thank you for enabling us to awaken this day,
to breathe, to see, to hear, think, and feel.
Thank you for inviting us to share life and love,
the ultimate miracle, with you!

Starling

I long to be like a starling,
one of a flock,
no ego but that of the energy,
the collective sense of purpose,
a living wave of bone, flesh, and feather
effortlessly changing direction.
Who guides where they fly or
to which tree they will roost for a moment?
A communal mind as they are startled all at once
and take flight again.
I long to be like a starling,
one of the many
in harmony with the will and energy that is life itself.

I vividly recall sitting at the park in prayer when a flock of starlings visited. I was awestruck and envious of their ability to fly in unison, rapidly altering direction, then resting for a while on the grass to forage. There is a deep desire within me to experience that sense of oneness with other people and with God.

Sixty Percent Water

Translucent, shining, glimmering,
reflective, brittle, transitory,
magnificent.

Flowing, healing medium,
primordial life matter,
emotions spanning rage to serenity,
seeking,
satisfying.

Ineffable, mysterious, boundless,
ever expanding and changing,
capable of union and integration,
yet still longing for more,
to change again,
for ultimate purpose.

Oh, how glorious the human person fully alive!

While having a patio breakfast at Ventana Inn and Spa overlooking the ocean near Big Sur, California, I was overcome with a sense of peaceful oneness with the ocean, and with God.

La Ventana (The Window)

Ocean
melts into the shore
melts into my heart
vast
timeless
gentle
beautiful
rhythmic
melts into the heavens
melts into my heart
unitive
complete
soothing
healing
alluring
melts into God
melts into my heart

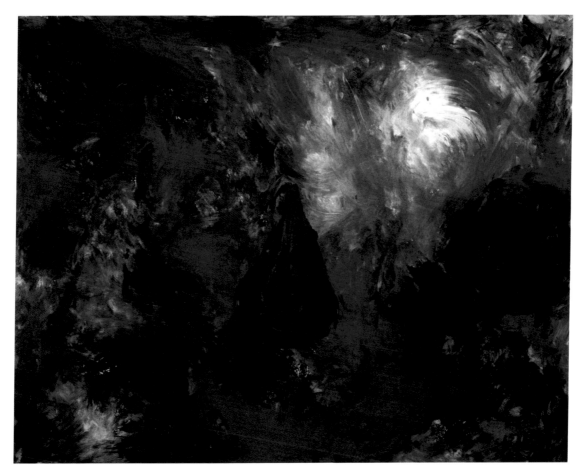

As a drop of water is to the ocean, so we are to God. God is our source and sustains our existence. We can become overwhelmed with how small we are compared to the vastness of creation, and even more, the Creator. At the same time, we can rejoice in that God lives within us.

Pulsing

In the trees seeming so stable and solid
and slowly growing,
in the grass,
in the cells of another person,
in molecules in a gaseous state,
in the matter of some distant star,
in what forms a black hole,
and even in a corpse,
the energy of God pulses …
 with life
 with invitation
 with hope
 with timelessness
 with expression
and in fleeting moments
I can almost come to the awareness
that my heart pulses in unison with God.

I Know What God Smells Like

I know what God smells like …
bald cypress trees in early winter,
cold, crisp mountain air,
a baby's head freshly shampooed,
red roses,
burgundy wine.
Do you ever stop to smell God?
If so, do you stop as often as you wish you would?
What a gift it is to smell,
the sense where memory resides.
Emanuel enters his world
amidst the smells of hay and dung and sheep,
of cold, crisp air.
God is with us to smell as we do, what we do.
God is with us as we smell love transformed into matter.
Praise God for the sense of smell!

Insects at the park. One time a fly was annoying me as I tried to focus on reading the Bible. Finally, I got the message to pay attention to the fly instead, and so I closed the book and marveled at how amazing my visitor was. No human could ever create such perfection with ease of flight, awareness of surroundings, and reaction time.

If I Were

If I were a duck
I would swim and fly
and travel from north to south
and back again.
If I were a dog,
I would bark and run
and pee on shrubbery and smile.
I would sniff all sorts of things and places
without a second thought,
perhaps without even a first thought.
If I were an ant,
I would carry a piece of bread
five times my size,
and I could never feel lost
because ants share a communal mind.
If I were a tree,
I would just be …
such freedom not to have to do anything,
simply to be.
And if I were able to be myself,
if I were able to be fully human,
I would love always and everywhere,
and when being in love,
I would reflect God by being
what I was meant to be,
as all of creation does.

Love Interest

As a love interest gives flowers to his hopeful,
so God gives us trees, grass, clouds,
starry nights, sweet rain,
and insects too ingenious to imagine.
"Oh, won't you please engage me?" God wishes.
As a five-year-old child hangs on his mother's
recognition of the paper-plate purse he has made,
so God desires us simply to notice—
"See what I made, just for you!"
Love expressed deeper than words,
with such vulnerability, innocence, and freedom.

Jumping Off the Earth

Did you ever try to jump off the earth?
It would be easier to do that than to be
separated from God,
because the power of gravity is but a taste
of the attractive force of God's love.

So much of the spiritual journey is about trusting and surrendering to God. One way I have practiced this is to pray lying on the ground facing up, imagining that rather than resting upon the earth, the earth is above me—holding me from falling into space. God never lets go.

I have never had such a deep, prolonged experience of beauty as I did while on retreat at Sacred Heart Jesuit Retreat House in Sedalia, Colorado. I wrote "Old Glory" on the fourth of July.

Old Glory

To look away would be a sin.
Surely, not stopping to watch
and take it in
would be refusing God's gracious invitation
into beauty, peace, awe, and wonder.
I'm so grateful for the colors …
glowing yellow,
radiant white,
hues of blues,
grays,
shadows,
and I especially love the pinks and purples …
How do you do that, God,
all those colors in one sky always changing?
Of course then I recall that I have
the gift of eyesight …
thank you again for that.

It becomes so clear that my purpose
at this moment
is simply to notice you,
to pay attention to you,
to receive and be grateful,
and when I do …
you are grateful as well.
I don't remember ever witnessing a sunset more beautiful.
Thank you for sharing it with me.

It was an especially beautiful autumn day, and as I was walking to theology class, I noticed the sky, the colorful leaves, and the deep red burning bushes. And it occurred to me that this is holy ground just as Moses experienced, that God is here too—among the fall colors and feelings, students and homeless persons.

Beauty

Most beauty is transitory:
    organic
    alive
    like a passing cloud
    a sunset
    a youthful personage
    even a marble masterpiece deteriorates over time
perhaps because it is easier to notice
or appreciate what is new or different,
perhaps because God is too creative
to fill all the spaces reserved for beauty,
perhaps to remind us that what lasts forever
exists in a realm just beyond
our perception and comprehension.
Oh God, I love you.
Oh God, I thank you,
for everything,
for every thing,
every person,
every experience,
and every encounter with beauty.

Chapel

There is a chapel in the park near my home
where God's Love pours out
along with the rain, sun, clouds, grass, trees,
insects, children's voices, and pervasive life energy.
God prays with me there,
like familiar lovers,
sometimes impassioned,
other times gently caressing,
and yet many times just being there together in silence,
not unlike an elderly couple sitting
or a dog with its steward resting leisurely.
Oh God, won't you please pray with me this day?
Won't you please play in me this moment?
Give me the grace to invite the space within myself
that is home to you.
Let the smile of my heart broaden to welcome your presence.
Let me breathe you in
that together we may breathe you out into the world.

Sometimes while praying in the park, I close my eyes and hold my face in my hands.
I become less aware of the beauty and life surrounding me, and enter more deeply
into the dark mystery of God.

Solar Powered

Sometimes when I pray
I remember that I am solar powered,
basking in the light and heat of the sun,
closed eyes seeing blazing orange with dancing stars,
skin that soaks in the energy, and psyche that is nourished.
Sometimes when I pray
I do indeed become open, passive, and oriented
enough toward God to purely receive the love,
not even thinking ahead to how this love will be
reflected or re-emitted through me in the future …
Why be concerned about what is as natural
as sitting in prayer on a sunny day?

In this painting I tried to capture the feeling of *Solar Powered*. I felt nourished by the energy and warmth of the sun. I felt God's desire for me to be alive. I felt grateful for so much. I sat on a bench outside a church welcoming and basking in those feelings.

Home

"The truly inspired can play."

A Trip

I closed my eyes and was transported to a remote planet,
where colors danced as from artistic genius,
where beauty abounded,
and gentleness pervaded all,
a place of tangible revelation of God,
calm and bursting with energy at the same time,
breathtaking and life-giving,
overwhelming yet reassuring.
Then I opened my eyes and I was still in that place.
I was home.

Real

Oh mysterious God
let our love be real …
  like skinning a knee on concrete
  like the smell of bread baking
  like the hearty hug of a close friend
  like an orgasm
  like the blinding light of the sun
Yes, let our love be real
and let it pour out into the world in abundance.

Start Close

When you ask "How can today be a loving day?"
start close,
with your spouse,
your children,
your parents,
your neighbors (the ones you enjoy least),
yourself,
and God.
Yes, start with God,
the source of all love.
Start with what touches you
so often you barely notice.
Perhaps it's your pet
or the flower potted on your front porch
or the tree you can see from your window—
ever present, ever changing.
Did you hear it whisper,
"Will you please love me?"
and did you notice how
faithfully that tree loves what is close to it—
the birds,
the insects,
the air,
and you?
Yes, I say, start close
and let love grow from there.

Threadbare

I've rubbed the fabric of God so often
that the threads poke out.
The words I spoke to a friend this morning
a stranger spoke to me in the afternoon.
What I long for, for another,
another longs for, for me.
And out of the shadow emerges the realization
that not only does God weave through my day, my life,
but also that I am a thread of God,
and integral to the fabric, both woven and weaver.
The thread pokes out that was always there …
> of comfort
> of refuge
> of being at home
> of holiness
> of playfulness
> of reverence
> of love
> of God
> and of myself in God.

The First Kindness

we receive before we can remember …
we give to a parent or sibling …
and now …
the first kindness is what we offer to ourselves.

Marilyn's Garden

quiet please
please quiet
in my sanctuary
my wholly place
without time
or worry
of God in my garden
and my garden in God
my bare hands in Mother Earth
playful dog
sprouting seeds
and weeds that whisper welcome
let me rest here
let me bask in life and freedom
let me be who I most want to be
alone with the ones I love

The Sunday after Thanksgiving was a holy day. Our daughter was sick
with a respiratory infection and had decided to stay home from college
one more day. And I recall what I was hoping for during Advent … to
rest in God, to rest with God, to welcome God resting in me … and to
welcome the gift of the present. This was her senior year of her bachelor's
degree, and she planned to marry in summer. Part of the gift is to
appreciate how numbered and precious are the days when she's home,
which I tried to capture in this poem.

Precious

Awakened by trio of bounding dog,
gentle daddy, and comforting mother.
Tender moaning—stay with us today.
Let us care for you this day.
Let us care for each other, and in so doing,
ourselves as well.

Doctor visit, swallow some pills,
recover in the kitchen.
Fragrance of onion, cheese, and sizzling.
Yes, love smells so good it can heal our souls.

Midday napping, trio in bed once again—
tender, touching, loving, sharing.
Relaxing the moment/movement of the day.
Savoring our time together, she asks
"Must you get old and die, Mommy?"

Dinner, and again time to welcome
the aroma of acceptance and laughter.
We must have chocolate for dessert
(to hell with the diet).

And bedtime, fresh hair smelling,
recounting today's hugs,
admitting that the routine will return tomorrow,
and thankful, so very thankful
for a day of healing and a life filled with love,
love expressed through family.

Over time I came to see that my own experience of God's love spread to all other aspects of my life, particularly personal relationships. I began to see that not only is each person a flower of God's love, but also a bush radiating that love to the world.

Wounded

A five-year-old boy
uncomfortable with everything …
his haircut,
his teeth,
his family,
himself,
stands silent with extended arms
in a fifty-three-year-old body,
too sad to speak,
not even knowing what he would say if he could,
longing for loving attention.
Believing that Jesus is embracing him,
yet not feeling it.
Believing that love can heal all wounds,
yet not feeling it.
Longing to be free of what is a big part of himself,
yet at the same time
not wanting to run
or hide
but instead celebrate his deepest self.

Who am I, Lord?
You are my beloved,
wounded,
cherished,
a source of my joy.
I suffer with you,
I suffer in you,
and I call you to greater freedom,
freedom, not forgetting,
forgiving,
accepting my love,
and the truth of our goodness
and adequacy.
I am with you in your brokenness
because it is my brokenness too.
Allow me to be resurrected through your triumph.
Praise the Risen Christ who lives through me!

My counselor suggested I revisit the most painful memories of my childhood in prayer and minister as an adult to myself as a child, with Jesus there. This painting depicts the sense of integration of my inner child with my adult self, with Jesus blessing and healing as the adult holds the child.

Sometimes we can feel "at home" when in another place ... if we are with someone who accepts us as we are, even if we are that someone.

Permission

I give you permission to be both/and instead of either/or,
masculine and feminine, black and white,
rich and poor, hard and soft,
grateful and angry (so angry you want to break something).

I give you permission to burn the box
that others try to keep you in
(here, borrow my matches).

I give you permission to talk about God and faith,
and also to talk about your questions and doubts
about God and religion (my, how you are growing).

I give you permission to believe that you
already are the person you most want to be,
deep down you are (and I can see it)
and I will offer you encouragement
to let that person rule your life.

I give you permission to remember
the tragedies of your childhood—
abandonment, ridicule, loneliness, abuse—
permission to be proud and ashamed,

to tell of your successes and failures.
Tell me about your kids and what makes you cry,
how you have hurt each other,
and how deeply you love each other.

I give you permission to tell me
the secret you think only you carry
(I bet it has something to do with fear,
inadequacy, un-love, un-acceptance)
and together we will find that our secrets
are not so very different.

I give you permission to touch me,
my heart, my hand, my body, my soul,
to discover that before all the hurts began
we were siblings.

I give you permission,
and when I give this gift to you
I give it to myself as well.

Sacrament

She prays in the kitchen
with holy water,
flour, sugar, and baking powder.
She delights in a few chips of chocolate.
The ritual music is jazz
because those who are truly inspired can improvise …
    music
    dance
    cooking
    living life
    loving
The truly inspired can play.
She celebrates the birth of her son
by preparing to celebrate at dinner,
and as her hands work
her heart whispers over and over
    Thank you God, for this child.
    Thank you for coming to me in this way.
    Thank you for allowing me to also give birth to love.
    Thank you God for this special day.

Love Today

The blind man who was healed
later got the flu,
argued with his wife,
died a painful death.
Oh, sweet Jesus, help me
to not be discouraged by
what may happen tomorrow
or fear the pain and suffering
that accompanies living,
but rather help me fully
cooperate with acting in love today.

How Often

How often
the person God
is most inviting
us to love
is ourselves.

Care Giver

Like a variety show act
I need to keep all the plates spinning
staying connected with friends
and those I love
and those who love me
caring for those who need my loving help
my presence, my ear, my hug.
Never mind the many other things
I must DO
or the things I wish
I could DO,
This is my DUTY, my purpose
is to live in this way …
But sometimes I get so tired
and then I rest in God.
I rest in God's embrace
giving care to me.

Family

"Thank you, gentle God, for loving me
as I am,
through the ones who know me best,
my family."

I Saw the Face of Jesus

I saw the face of Jesus,
and to my surprise
He didn't have long hair and a beard.
He didn't look like Mother Teresa
or Martin Luther King Jr.,
or like the beggar I encountered yesterday.
I saw the face of Jesus
in my wife and children,
the ones who hear me fart,
bear the brunt of my crabbiness,
moan at my corny humor,
the ones I hug
and who hug me back.
Thank you, gentle God, for loving me
as I am,
through the ones who know me best,
my family.

Kindness

Random acts of kindness toward strangers are quite wonderful.
Random acts of kindness toward people we know—
now that is really something.

The Hug

Do you know those times when you walk into the kitchen,
and your beloved is busy cooking,
and you turn her toward you,
and as she consents,
a hug and a tender kiss,
and more hugging,
just being,
time stopping for a moment,
slightly rocking together as one—
that is what prayer is like for me.

Or when your young child rests on your lap,
perhaps to read to you or with you,
or just to talk about whatever,
and deep in your heart,
sometimes deeper than consciousness,
you know how precious and holy this encounter is,
smelling her hair,
rubbing her back,
kissing her forehead,
time stopping for a moment,
slightly rocking together as one—
that is what prayer is like for me.

I like to say that people are flowers of God's love. Like every flower, each person is unique and beautiful. Each is a physical revelation of God, the source of all goodness and life. The marks flying around represent that our goodness touches the lives of many other people, in ways we recognize and in ways we do not.

I was having a cup of coffee by myself in a restaurant, and all of a sudden I became aware of the deep, profound love I have for my son. Thank you God.

A Taste

God gave me another taste of heaven today.
Sitting in a restaurant
suddenly
yet so gently
aware
aware
of the deep beauty
profound beauty
and goodness
of my son
his smile
his energy
his sense of justice
his passion
and the tears flowed
awareness that my only response could be and was
gratitude
so deep that voices cannot make it sound
silent
holy song of angels
where "Thank you" can only be expressed
with the depths of my being.

I am gratitude
I am in God
I am in heaven
through this gift of awareness
God is revealed to Godself
through me, to me,
and I receive confirmation
that my eternal purpose is to be an angel.

This is my family (including me), blossoming flowers of God's love, unique, united, and growing. The background of black and white represents the dark mystery of God and the light of Love, ever spiraling. What type and color of flower are you? What are your special beauties?

Because I Have Faith

When my wife got sick
and our lives were turned upside down
and the freedom I had grown so accustomed to was gone,
and when I had to watch her cry
in pain and fear and suffering,
because I have faith, I asked
"Where are you in this situation, God?"

When I was repulsed by segregation and complacency
and my judging attitude and cynicism
and the exercise of power over the powerless,
and when a sense of confusion and impotence overwhelmed me,
because I have faith, I asked
"Where are you in this situation, God?"

And then God reminded me that when gazing at the sunset
I don't ask this question—
not because I don't have faith,
but because God's presence is so apparent.
And then I realized that the answer is always the same,
that where God is, is with me, with us,
always, and in all ways.
Always encouraging and inviting us to more.
When witnessing a sunset,
to stop and soak it in,
to receive the healing and wholeness beauty offers.

When facing pain and loss,
to surrender,
to let go and trust that God is suffering with us,
and to know that whatever we are
and whatever we do is enough.
When disturbed by injustice,
to act out of courage and love,
to trust my heart
and to speak what I believe is the truth.

The death of our beloved dog was both profoundly sad and profoundly beautiful at the same time (because of the love being shared). The experience became so powerful that I felt I was outside of myself observing.

On a Dime

A glorious day
beautiful weather
feeling very alive
like everything will land butter side up.
Then a call
in pain
in tears
helpless daughter
and mother and father.
Numbness eventually yields
to deep sadness and sorrow.
One day changed in a moment.
Yet the world is the same
and the meaning of life is the same.
What changed is the color of love
like a kaleidoscope turning.
And so love remains,
always.
And love leads to suffering,
always.
And suffering can lead to freedom and joy,
but will it this time,
and if so when,
and what color will it be?

Lost

Today I lost something precious.
When I had the urge to hug,
I let it pass unfulfilled.
When I could have smiled,
I looked inward and resisted.
When I could have listened,
I allowed busyness to steal me away.
I can live with that,
I do each day, with the hope
of a tomorrow more filled with love.
But what I cannot bear to face,
what stops my heart,
is the thought of losing you.

Split Moment

I awoke to silence
and for a split moment strained to listen,
wondering whether my world had ended.
Then I heard her exhale
and so myself.

Selfless Pride

As her child nestles at the breast,
she experiences indescribable intimacy,
clarity of purpose,
gratitude, and selfless pride.

As the toddler takes the first step,
rides a bike,
writes her name,
reads to her father,
accomplishes what previously was beyond her capabilities,
as she grows stronger and wiser and even more beautiful,
her mother beams,
every part of her explodes with gratitude, hope,
joy, and selfless pride
for the part of her that could never have been,
but now is.

And as she feels the child kick in the womb of her daughter,
even larger emotion swells,
for someone else to experience what comes with
giving, nurturing, loving, and rejoicing in another life.

And throughout this timeless snapshot of a few decades,
repeated for millennia,
God smiles with tears of joy.
Oh, Mother God,
it is no wonder the universe continues to expand,
else your selfless pride could not be contained.

No Accidents

With the Mother Father God
there are no unintended pregnancies,
but rather the life of each person
is first born in God's heart,
and gestation occurs with a yearning for that life
that pales in comparison to that of Abraham and Sarah.
So the joy of new parents is but a hint
of the joy God takes in each person,
each beloved child, each moment.
Our existence was premeditated
and the love of our life forever promised.

Seduction

From the very beginning you seduced us,
with beauty
and goodness
and abundance,
with diversity
and freedom
and with the sense of being incomplete.
You seduced us by so easily demonstrating
the impossible—
not one, but two amazing pregnancies,
and you are so clever and subtle
(skills imperative for a master seductress)
because you came as one irresistible.
Surely, no mother can resist to embrace
and nurture a young, vulnerable infant.
And the seduction continues beyond what we recognize,
as naked bodies caress,
as beauty cannot avoid seeping
(and often pouring out) through nature,
as you accompany us in our darkness,
and as you unceasingly invite us to more
than we appreciate.

Making Love

To stop asking,
to stop seeking to know more fully,
to stop welcoming surprise,
is to presume that we fully know the other—
who by definition is not fully knowable—is to deflate wonder
and stifle the purpose of entering into the mystery
of deep relationship.

In the Bedroom

waiting
loving
sitting on the edge of the bed
gazing upon us
naked bodies
smelling us
sensual savoring
delighting in the love We share
delighting in how that love will
grow and be expressed and received
while delighting in the love that is present
resisting the urge to awaken us
smiling like a mother at sleeping infant
patient
loving
waiting

Familiar Bedfellows

I went to bed with God
and in early morning hours
my wife showed up,
naked, cozy, alluring the cuddle,
and half-dreaming,
half in the sanctuary of safety and possibility.
I savored the moment,
welcomed them with gratitude,
and prayed love upon her.
My soul sang as she slept
only half-aware of our nestling in God.

I went to supper with my wife
and God showed up,
not just in the thirty-second ritual prayer,
but more deeply and warmly in her compassion
and loving care for our children,
and in God's desire for her
to experience a larger taste of God's presence,
and in God's desire for her
continued healing and greater freedom and joy,
and we all laughed with dessert.

And now alone in church,
not alone at all
because they are so very present with me,
really present,
not just in my memory, heart, or body,
but the Love is present,
and so again I savor
and welcome
and rejoice,
cuddling with them.

Awakening

As I awaken,
near my dear one,
I realize,
that where I most long to be,
I AM.
Thank you so much.
Thank you so much.

Jesus

"I do not call you servants any longer, because the servant does not know what the master is doing; but I have called you friends, because I have made known to you everything that I have heard from my Father." (John 15:15)

"In the beginning was the Word, and the Word was with God, and the Word was God … And the Word became flesh and lived among us, and we have seen his glory …" (John 1:1, 14)

The Word

We don't have to try too hard
to imagine how we may suffer
in the future
through loss in myriad forms
through pain
through sinfulness
perhaps we may even find ourselves
in the place of suffering now
and we are so thirsty for relief
even for a moment,
yet that may not come.
But in the end the last word will be Love.
Love will have the last word.
Love was the first word
and is our hope as we face suffering.
Praise you, Jesus—now and forever!

An artist and spiritual director friend and I spent three hours together, looking at and talking about many of my paintings. Driving home from that meeting I made the commitment to pursue getting published. Shortly afterward, I wrote the following poem. Thank you, Annette.

Medium

Sweet Jesus, did you carve statues of the saints in your life,
the ones whom you admired and who inspired you most?
Did you create beautiful objects as a form of prayer,
to celebrate beauty, to co-create with God?
Did your creativity spill out into painting,
drawing, poetry, or music?
Were you good in the kitchen, baking and cooking creations
around which love would be celebrated and shared?
Are you creating through me now, through my life,
my work, my play, my prayer, my desires?
No question all the relationships in my life are colored,
are created and sustained in you.
Are you keeping some secret scrapbook
that you will show me in heaven,
and do you anticipate with excitement what we will create today?

And so I ask that I may never thwart your creative energy
out of resistance or fear,
but rather let your love be expressed through me
to weave a tapestry of joy in the world.
Praise you, Jesus—now and forever!

I was praying in an old church, staring at a statue of Mary holding the dead body of her son. After a while, it struck me that the sculptor included nipples on Jesus' body, and I wondered why. It was because Jesus was human just like us.

Jesus

He had nipples.
He enjoyed a good bowel movement.
He liked to bite his fingernails.
He enjoyed the exertion of his muscles
and the sweatiness that comes with accomplishment.
He had body odor,
yet sometimes his hair smelled so sweet.
Dust would cake between his toes.
He felt incomplete.
He felt limited.
He ached for this world to be more.
He experienced exhaustion and sickness,
loss and grief.
He cried …
not only from his eyes,
but from his heart.
His heart sobbed at times,
wailing, moaning,
in the darkness until the tears ran dry
and the pain subsided into deep sadness.

He was a good friend and still is.
He liked wine, flavorful food, and conversation.
He yearned for union and intimacy
more profound than sex,
and he knew how to invite and allow it.

He understood that nothing is useless,
even nipples on a man,
that nothing is so desperate or desolate
that God is truly absent
or that hope and love become impossible.
He experienced the amazing and enormous power of love
and came to know that under that power
nothing, absolutely nothing
is unable to be the seed for new life, hope, and joy.

So, Dear Lord, thank you for the useless nipples in my life,
the experiences of the mundane,
and the periods of desolation
because with your love
they will blossom beyond what I can imagine.

Parousia Paradox

Christ Jesus, once raised you haven't changed.
Eternity is forever, and as I understand it, unchanging.
Yet, according to all accounts,
those with prior knowledge did not recognize you at first—
a fellow traveler,
a cook on the shore,
a gardener.
So I wonder, when you come again,
will you need a shave and a haircut?
Or will you be more inconspicuous,
wearing blue jeans, sneakers, and a baseball cap?
Will you need to lose more than a few pounds?
Could you stand to have your teeth fixed?
Will you look more like the Pope or the homeless man?
Or perhaps the grandma who has learned
what really matters in life …
acceptance, love, family, sharing of good food,
and sharing of self?
Will you be eager to fish again,
to smell the sea,
or feel a piece of wood in your hands?—
happy and painful memories associated with wood, I know.
Please don't come looking like President Bush,
or those who rape our earth so precious.
I'd rather that you took the appearance
of the neighbor who irritates me,
or the stranger I fear.
And if you will,
let your second coming be through me,
yet—true to the paradox—
I will not claim as me
what others recognize as you.

Seeing with the Eyes of Jesus

If I could see with the eyes of Jesus,
how beautiful the world would be!
Seeing the goodness, deep loving God-ness
within all life, enveloping me.
Seeing the incompleteness, the sadness,
emptiness, the dismay, yet knowing that the
rhythm of life is somehow complete in this way.
Loving it all, en-livening it all
around those eyes that see with a heart burning white.
If I could see with the eyes of Jesus,
such a joy to be in others' company.
So much to love, so much energy to live.
Alive, tender, alive and tender.
And it's for others that I hope to see with Love's eyes,
to be a vehicle of joy, or forgiveness, or healing or empathy.
Still, I'm often surprised at how joyful joy can be,
and that the eyes of Jesus see not only others,
but also see me.

On a bustling Saturday morning on Chicago's Magnificent Mile, I did not miss a step when tucking a twenty-dollar bill into the empty cup of a man begging. When I was about thirty feet from him, I heard a loud "Thank you, man!" and we became connected. No one else noticed as we mediated Jesus to each other.

All Wrong

Every one I have ever seen is wrong.
Every crucifix has Jesus clothed.
Surely this is inaccurate,
as sure as it is more humiliating
to be naked amidst the jeers,
the badgering, the outright hatred,
and the violence of heart that is fueled in mobs
and deeply rooted in fear.
Surely he was naked to the world,
and naked before God.
Wasn't that what got him into so much trouble
in the first place?
His fearless desire and discipline of standing
naked before God …
abiding naked in Their midst,
and before and with people as well,
a naked lover and healer and revealer of truth.
He was so filled with love that fear and violence
had no room in him,
none at all.
Absolutely none.

Have you ever been able to love that deeply?
To trust and surrender so fully that fear had no room?
To lay down your life because love did not
permit any alternative?

Even the thought of love this profound—
even the thought—
is so frightening for us that we put a loin cloth
on our naked savior, redeemer, lover God.
Are we ashamed of his humanness?
Are we afraid to gaze upon the type of surrender
that deep love can yield?

Let us ask forgiveness not only for hiding ourselves from God,
but also for hiding the depth of God's love from ourselves.
Oh, sweet lover Jesus, let us stand naked
before each other that we may let go
of all and any obstacles to love,
that we may let go of pride and desire for honor,
that we may abandon all of ourselves
completely and totally to you.
Praise you, Jesus—now and forever!

During peer supervision (when a colleague helped me process after the fact my experience of giving spiritual direction to someone), I got in touch with a deep sense of sadness from my childhood. During that session, I felt as though I was being cradled by Jesus. Now, in prayer I sometimes return to that image.

The Fullness of Being Human

If the essence of a human being is the capacity to love,
didn't Jesus reveal the fullness of being human?
He loved God.
He loved himself.
He loved his neighbor (who he defined as all other people).
He loved to the point of being tortured and murdered,
and through all this,
he never once stopped loving.

Did he ever fear?
After all, love pushes out fear.
So in the garden when he anguished,
this perhaps was dread,
suffering (wishing things to be different),
but never fear
because he always loved
(and he always does)
and he always chose to rely upon God.

When he was angry,
or even violent in the temple,
it was out of love.
When he encountered people—
poor, lame, wealthy, arrogant, hateful,
the emptiness of being human—
it always was in love,
with love.
Oh, my friend Jesus loved people,
he loved life,
he loved a party,
and he loves us, each of us,
as we are,
and he always, always will.

Touched

When I recall that Jesus
refused not to touch anyone
I realize that he longs
to touch me,
So I say yes once again.

Once in prayer, I entered the story of the woman suffering from hemorrhages—as that woman. "Immediately aware that power had gone forth from him, Jesus turned about in the crowd and said, 'Who touched my clothes?'" (Mark 5:30)

I was praying at the park one summer day and noticed a mother with her young child on the playground. Then the following poem came to me.

Mother

She wiped his toddler nose
and held his hand
and told him stories as he sat on her lap,
stories of the ancestors,
ancient and recent,
stories of her childhood.
She expressed her joy and love and gratitude
to him through her actions and words
and in her prayers.
She delighted in the times he
and her husband spent together,
learning how to saw and carve and nail,
and how to invite God into everyday work,
to begin and end the day the same way—in prayer.
Her husband taught him about growing into a man,
gentle, respectful, generous.
She expected him to become a preacher,
a rabbi, a leader, or a combination,
but not a revolutionary.
Yet her biggest surprise was that at his essence

he was a lover.
He could melt hearts,
dissipate fear,
and heal hatred
in those brave enough to spend time with him.
And she knew his parents
had not taught this precious gift,
although they welcomed and encouraged it.
No, this most precious, essential gift
was Godself living in him,
a gift he shared so freely,
a gift that we all have been given,
a gift we are challenged to accept and to live.

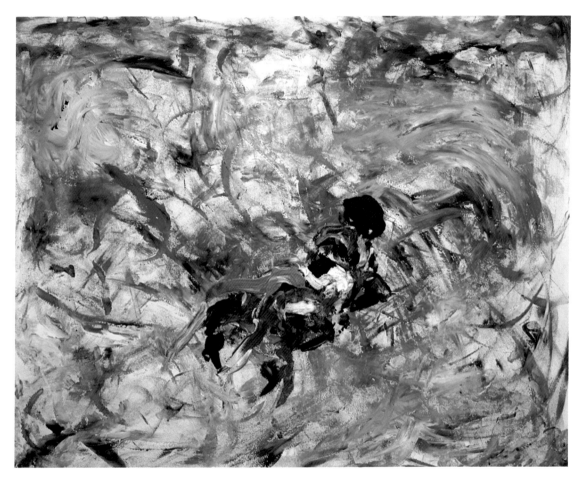

During prayer I experienced a strong desire to be close to Jesus, so I imagined resting my head on Jesus' chest, as I suppose the Beloved Disciple did. This was such an experience of peace, intimacy, acceptance, and timelessness.

Comfortable Clothes

Jesus wore comfortable clothes …
sandals,
a loose-fitting tunic,
a beard,
a smile,
an uninhibited sense of humor,
an aura of love, acceptance, and peace,
an ease with kindness, generosity, and intimacy.

Dear Lord, let your loving presence
be at home in me …
warm like the sun on my skin,
bright like a full moon on a clear black night,
gentle as a kiss on the palm,
fertile as dark soil,
and sweet as the most fragrant flowers.
Let others encounter your loving presence
through me.
Let me be and do in harmony with you
each moment this day.

Perhaps one of the most profound sentences in the Gospels is one of the shortest, "Jesus began to weep." (John 11:35)

Right to Die

He was there when Joseph died.
Word had reached him in time to return home,
to be a consoling presence to his mother,
his father, and those who would mourn his passing.
It can be clear that there is a time for death,
and this clarity comes
through the graces of faith, hope, and love
in many dimensions and expressions.
Perhaps recalling this experience is what brought
him to tears outside the tomb of his dear friend Lazarus.
It was a time when there were no words
but instead silence and numbness.
He was grateful to be there for them
and for himself, and for the glory of God
that shone so powerfully in this darkness,
and in the rituals of preparation and resolution—
anointings, confessions, crying, laughing,
holding hands, praying, and sitting empty.
Yes the silence of God was so very present at his father's death,
silence filled with compassion, hope, trust, and gratitude.
Returning to God the life God gave to the world
can be so very right.
Praise you, Jesus—now and forever!

Holy Communion

"… because no smile exists in isolation."

I Say Yes

Today I say yes to being the medium
through which God is revealed.
Today I accept that …
    I am both the beloved who is other,
    somehow separate and distant enough from God
    to be in relationship with God,
    separate enough to be cherished
    for the unique person I am,
    separate enough to be free (at least potentially)
    to be the delight of God.
        and
    I exist within God,
    the core of my existence is God,
    separation is impossible,
    anything I may label as mine (even consciousness)
    exists in communion with God.
    For God not to love me would mean that
    God would not love Godself.
    God and I have the same DNA.
    I breathe in God.
    I breathe out God.
    I am the breath of God
    and God is the breath of me.

I say yes to my limitations
that narrow my consciousness,
that inhibit my cooperation,
that prevent God from being more completely revealed.

I say yes to God's glory,
evident through my goodness,
love,
beauty,
vulnerability,
compassion,
joy.

I say yes to the mystery,
of constant invitation,
life without beginning or ending,
concurrent suffering and rejoicing,
the completeness of the present moment,
constant expansion,
perfect imperfection.

I say yes to love,
to relationship,
community,
family,
authentic church,
God,
and myself as the revelation of God!

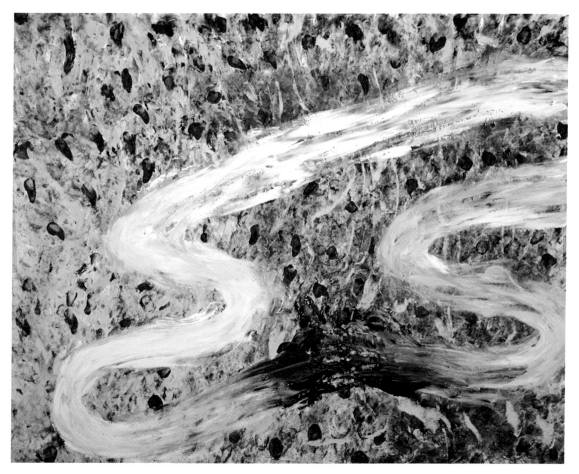

Since each person is a revelation of God, God meets Godself through the flesh of people. Have you experienced moments when this type of holy encounter becomes obvious, perhaps through a sense of love, joy, peace, or friendship—a moment when there was no doubt God was present?

Interplanetary

There is a person in another galaxy
thinking of me.
The form of her body
and its color are unknown on earth.
We are connected by our desire to
be aware that we are connected.
We smile at each other through
this desire
and through the connection,
because no smile exists in isolation.

Intersection

The intersection of God and me …
   is my body
   is my awareness
   are my thoughts
   are my holy desires
   is goodness
   is organic
   is beautiful
The intersection of God and me
is passing away yet coming into being.
And complete union between God and me already exists,
although I do not yet experience it.

Drop Noodle

I am like a drop noodle,
of the same stuff as my source,
yet unique in form,
a special expression of what is.
I am created separate enough to "see" my source,
to be aware of the Other who originates all.
I am the will that can choose to see, ignore,
run away, or hide from this Other who is God.
My essence is awareness (consciousness)
and choice—the rest is an expression of me.
And this will and consciousness are but
an expression of the One.
Then the more I am truly aware—really aware of anything—
the more authentic I become,
the holier I become.
And then the more often I choose,
the more intentional I am,
again, the holier I become.
With your help, dear Lord and Lover,
let me be aware of you
and your glorious presence in everything—
surely your presence is in all.
This is what I choose, over and over and over again.

Often I have prayed for the grace that I may receive what God wishes to give and that God may receive all of me into Godself. It is a time of embracing my deepest desire (which comes from God) and admitting my powerlessness to cause the union I crave. It is a time to trust God once again.

Seeping

Of all the ways God seeps out through my life,
I suppose I do have a favorite.
It's not the tears
or the hugs
or the writings,
the prayer times
or acts of generosity
or the compassion of listening.
No. It's in the ways obscured to me.
Because my hope is that these are
the ways most efficacious and ubiquitous.
These are the ways when my ego has surrendered.
These are the ways when the essence of me
and the essence of God are most deeply in communion.

Missing

I am missing the sensual experiences,
deep colors and piercing smells,
the warmth of the sun.
I am missing the woods and its organic embrace.
I am missing the exhilaration of passion and call and mission.
I am missing the presence of a companion on the journey.
Surely I am missing countless invitations and opportunities
as I look down into the silence of me.
I can no longer feel the pounding in my chest.
I am missing you, oh God,
and so I am also missing myself.

Is it so wrong to wish for annihilation into you,
to want this life to end
so that what I perceive as separation from you will end?
Aren't you the one who puts the longing into my heart
for your presence,
for union,
and don't you also long for union with me?
Does logic dictate that we are already united
or that the union we crave comes only through a process,
that the craving is like the water and sun and time
that enable a flower to blossom?
Oh God, I surrender all to you,
these longings, these questions, my future, and myself.

In the Flesh

I understand that you long for the experience of insights
or consoling feeling,
dreams or visions.
I know you long for a spiritual message,
inner peace,
acceptance,
and assurance regarding your choices.
But I must say, dear one,
and please hear me,
if you wish to encounter God,
touch another person.
My favorite, most blessed medium for revelation
is the human being.
And know also that you are called
to claim your place among those chosen
to enflesh transcendence.

*Hungry for experience of communion with God, and with other people
at an essential level, we are powerless to make it happen. But we can
embrace our desire … and wait … and welcome the gift if it be granted.
We received one such gift at a dinner with our daughter, her roommate,
and roommate's parents after a music recital. Though it was only the
second or third time we had met, we were surprised to find ourselves
deeply, spiritually connected—not because we were talking about God
or faith, but because we were being our true selves.*

Holy Communion

party of six
pitcher of sangria
tapas, the food of tasting and sharing
grace overcame us
and our souls connected
before we could realize
we all knew this moment
would not last
nor could be recreated
so we chose to honor it
surrender to it
sharing ourselves
sharing our hearts
engaging in holy communion

Every Little Bit

Every little bit,
I offer every little bit to you, my Lord.
Every cell, every hair,
every thought, every fear,
every desire, every heartbeat,
every breath,
even what I try to hide from myself—
I offer that to you as well.
Take me.
Receive all of me into you.
Let us become one.
Let whatever of me that is separate
from you be annihilated.
Let me enter completely into the freedom of your love,
the compassion of your suffering,
the joy and hope you know.
Let our hearts smile together.
Let me see your face in the mirror.
Let me claim and give away your love
over and over again.

Let me proclaim your truth—
not my truth, but your truth.
Let me awaken each day with thoughts of you.
Let me thank you for yet another invitation
to love and be loved,
to enter into and be subsumed within love.
That is your truth, isn't it?
Let your gentleness fill me and pour out into the world;
use me as a fountain.
Let me melt into you
and you melt into me.
Inseparable and indistinguishable lovers,
now and always.

Fell into God

I fell completely into God
and afterward I met a friend
and asked if she noticed anything different.
She said, "No. You look completely like yourself."

I tried to express an experience of dissipating into God—fulfilling, unfulfilling, fleeting, and sustaining all at the same time. "For now we see in a mirror, dimly, but then we will see face to face. Now I know only in part; then I will know fully, even as I have been fully known." (1 Cor 13:12)

The term "Eucharist" is derived from the Greek word meaning "thanksgiving."

Thanksgiving

I welcome the drink of your life into mine.
I crave the physical union you long for with me.
Let your life blood permeate all of me …
my mind,
    my heart,
    my will,
    my bones,
    my eyes,
    and my skin.
Impregnate the womb of my heart.
And as your energy radiates from my core,
let it not be limited by my physicality,
but rather let the energy that became united as us
color the world with …
    love,
    acceptance,
    peace,
    joy,
    kindness,
    generosity,
    and beauty.
Enrapture me as only impassioned lovers can.
Let me accept that you cherish me as I am.

Melt my resistance with a wet kiss
that you may find me ever more open
and surrendered to you.
And let me be always grateful.

At Mass, anticipating receiving Holy Communion, I want to dive completely into God. After receiving, I imagine that Jesus caught me (as a child) and held me for a while. This evolved into Jesus and me engaged as best friends (me as adult). Finally, Jesus leaving, with me looking forward to our next encounter.

Reflecting on my desires and experiences of receiving Holy Communion,
I am in touch with the senses of longing and anticipation as well as the
reality of physical union with Christ. When walking up and back to
receive, I place my hands over my heart.

Closer

Again our eyes meet
and you choose to prick your finger
—gentle, peaceful surrender, anticipation and deep longing—
one drop of blood pools on your skin
and then I caress your wound, your opening,
in my mouth
—tears, acceptance, intimacy—
my turn to shed and share my life blood with you,
and the rhythmic exchange completes its first cycle.

Your hand on my heart.
I can feel its warmth and the pressure on my skin
—pulsating love, unceasing, without origin or end—
and then another cycle completed
with my hand on your chest,
increasing our awareness
that our energies are synchronized.
—wanting more, the fire of desire for deeper union
melts resistance—

You are holding my heart in your hand
and I am holding yours in mine,
motionless but for the beating,
pulsing love-longing to be even closer,
even closer still.
—speechless union of the essence of each other,
in you I AM, in me YOU ARE—
pulsing love-longing to be even closer,
even closer still.

During an imaginative prayer, Jesus and I exchange hearts. "… and it is no longer I who live, but it is Christ who lives in me. And the life I now live in the flesh I live by faith in the Son of God, who loved me and gave himself for me." (Gal 2:20)

One evening while having dinner alone in a fast food restaurant, I
noticed a woman with her young daughter. I was pierced by the beauty
of that mother-and-child scene, its holiness, its revealing of God …
and I started to cry. I went straight home and continued the experience
through prayer. In that time, two persons of the Holy Trinity came to me
and the Holy Spirit flowed between the three of us.

My God

She comes as a child
my God does
innocent, vulnerable
beautiful, dependent
honest, open
using simple words
wanting only to be with me
to cling to me
as I caress her
She comes to me this way

He comes as a friend
a companion who understands
who offers support, not judgment
encouragement
and who rejoices in my growth
in me becoming more
    free
    joy-filled

beloved
whole
myself

They bring tears when they visit
and feelings too profound to express
when they come
gratitude wells
in every cell of my being
and I can hear the gentle
cry from deep within my soul
saying "take me"
yet they already have

It comes with …
there are no words.
Haven't you seen it?
Haven't you experienced the surprise of God
on the horizon of your heart?
it's OK to believe it

If you let go of the ego and fear
if you trust once again
if you come like a child
you can cling to her
as she caresses you

In this painting, *My God,* I am kneeling while two members of the Holy Trinity dance around me and the Holy Spirit moves through us all. Perhaps the white circle enveloping this experience recalls the image of the communion host.

When serving as coordinator for a Week of Guided Prayer retreat,
I spend much of my time sitting in the gathering space of a church,
welcoming people as they come and go, chatting occasionally, sometimes
praying or writing down what may come to me. During one of these
days, a very deep sense of peace and unity with God came over me,
similar to the experience of gazing at the ocean near Big Sur, California.
We were there each day for one week. An administrator who worked at
the church left town unexpectedly on that Wednesday. She later told me
that when she returned the following Monday, she could feel the sense
of peace that lingered there even after we had left. I had not relayed my
experience to her.

Waves

The words "I Love You"
wash over me and through me
and in me
so very gently
this must be of God
rhythmically they come
like breathing
and I cannot distinguish which one of us is speaking
God or me
it's like we are both speaking through
the same medium of my consciousness
we speak the words to each other in union
and then the words shift to "Thank You"
and gratitude swells yet the gentleness remains

and then we go deeper into silence
becoming so purely gentle there are no words
then after a while "I Love You" returns

I do love You—I do.

It's like the gentleness of the ocean lives within me.
I welcome You, oh God.
I surrender all to You.

In this painting, can you see the image of me becoming one with the waves? "And the peace of God, which surpasses all understanding, will guard your hearts and your minds in Christ Jesus." (Phil 4:7)

If I paint the same experience about which I write, the painting follows the writing, which follows the experience. Except for the following Discontent. *I had intended to paint God and me staring lovingly at each other in prayer. First I painted myself. Then when I started to paint God's face, I realized I was painting myself in the womb of God.*

Discontent

I am a discontented fetus in the womb of God,
eager to embark on the next adventure,
eager to grow,
eager to be able to open my eyes and see God's face,
eager to wrap my arms around God's gentle index finger.
Oh loving God, thank you for keeping me safe,
for nurturing me with your love.
Thank you for always inviting me to more,
into deeper friendship, relationship, and partnership with you.
I long for the mutuality that emerging from your womb
will allow, and I know you yearn for that as well.
Even the thought of it delights you like an expectant mother.
Give me the grace to trust your perfect timing.
Let me come to know you ever more deeply,
from inside of you,
that I will always dwell in you
as your life dwells in me.

What a gift it is to be surprised by God, and in this particular instance, for God to reveal through my surrendered self the intimacy of our relationship as that of a fetus in the womb. Yet I long for more, as expressed in *Discontent*.

During prayer on another retreat, I had the experience of being in the
darkness of God, and that there was a hole in God's heart that only I
could fill. I stepped in.

A Holy Heart

There is a hole in God's heart
that only I can fill
perfectly and completely fill
only by me
only with me
as I am
nothing added
nothing missing
just me
completing the hole in God's heart
So I walk forward and step inside
drawn like a magnet
until our boundaries melt away
there is fusion
and closure
and beating of the one heart
In the dark completeness of God
we complete each other
hugging souls
and ecstasy
in the dark there is ecstasy

My experience of God as mystery is an experience of darkness, and I have come to feel comfortable there. In this painting, *A Holy Heart*, can you see the heart of God in the darkness?

One night sitting alone in church, I contemplate the consecrated host in the tabernacle, Jesus' love of people, the desire for union, and the sacredness of physical existence.

Let Me Out

How lonely it would be if Jesus had to remain only in church.
How sad indeed.
All alone most every night,
with only a holy night light for companionship.
A cold, isolated, sterile existence,
longing for connection with that
oh so blessed messiness of real life
people
instruments of joy and hatred,
serenity and violence,
fear and hope.
Not confined to remain lily white and pure,
untouched behind the locked golden doors,
but instead dirty,
smudged with the earth,
that first and fundamental connection,
humanity's ordained origin.
Plow your love into our hearts, Sweet Jesus,
into our flesh, bones, and blood.

Let your love continue to fill the earth through your people.
Enable us to claim our rightful place as humus,
the fertilizer of love.
Let us always remain grounded in you.

In The End

In the end, will it be exactly as we had expected,
or will it be entirely surprising,
or will it be both?
I don't want to die in my sleep.
I want to jump off a cliff into Jesus' arms.
I want to work at dying.
I want to participate in the process of letting go,
the ultimate surrender,
the final act of loving trust.
I look forward to that convergence of
deep sadness, hope, joy, and freedom,
enveloped in love and tenderness.

Notice I did not mention peace—
no resting on my deathbed;
total surrender is an active disposition.
And so as with all things future,
they begin in the present.
I have started to die as a way of living more fully.
Oh, surely I will be surprised,
God is much too creative and mischievous to forego that.
So perhaps exactly what I wish to avoid will be the gift
I will be offered—or just the opposite—
or in the end some of both.

Church

"… we are connected across time, …
not only through the structure of the church,
but not separate from it either."

Born Into It

Sometimes the greatest experiences of separation,
isolation, and rejection we feel precisely in
the place where we are supposed to feel
unconditionally loved, accepted, nurtured, and safe.

Sometimes we find ourselves feeling like babies
who were inadvertently switched
in the hospital nursery.

And sometimes it is the place
where we feel we most belong,
are most complete,
become our best selves.

Family.
Church.
Humanity.

Like a Child

I saw a three-year-old receive Holy Communion,
and it made me wonder …
what does that child comprehend about this experience,
and what is his experience of this holy encounter?
Doesn't Jesus give himself to all people,
including children,
including those who don't grasp the mystery?
I think I comprehend the experience more deeply
than that child, but let me not pretend for a moment
that I even begin to understand.
If this child is too young, when will he be old enough?
And so I feel like the apostles who shooed away
the children from Jesus–
mistaken, presumptuous, taught another lesson.
When will I ever come to understand the mystery that isn't …
that all are welcome, no exceptions?

I was inspired to write this while visiting a church in rural Missouri.
A church of good people, yet I felt as a stranger.

Is It a Catholic Thing?

I sit in the
              middle
                     of the pew
leaving room for others to be
with me and me with them.
Is it the sense of control,
perhaps a sense imperceptible by most,
that motivates people to sit on the end—
like they actually need to be able to rush out
in the middle of liturgy due to a medical condition?
Oh I pray that it is not intentional separation,
I just don't want to believe that.
I love that song "All are Welcome"
but not just because it is inclusive of all people
regardless of theology or denomination or race or gender,
but because it is about *welcoming*.

Do I make people who may sit next to me,
perhaps inadvertently because the end of my pew
had been unoccupied,
do I make them feel welcome?

And do they welcome me
and am I open to accepting the invitation if they give it?

Oh, how I long to hold the hand of whoever is next to me
as we pray the Lord's Prayer together.
I think if they really knew how I felt
they could not resist by looking straight ahead,
pretending not to notice my glance toward them.
Yet perhaps they feel the same toward me.
It is sad but true that it can be
a scary, uncomfortable feeling for some … holding hands.

Dear Lord, send your Spirit to enliven the sense of joy,
acceptance, and welcoming.
Let your love melt away my sense of separation and judgment.
Let me truly believe, and in fact see, that each person
is an expression of you,
and let me live from this reality.
Let us share hearts, hold hands, hug each other,
and yes even be oblivious to where we sit
because all are welcome in your love.
All are welcome.

This meditation came to me while I was sitting alone in a beautiful, mini-cathedral-style church in South St. Louis City, Our Lady of Sorrows Catholic Church. When it was built, all its members walked to church, neighboring Catholic churches were constructed as close as a mile apart, and all children walked to school. A time long past, yet the church continues to serve a vibrant faith community. I met someone there who had been a parishioner for eighty years.

Holy Souls

The holy souls are here,
in the flickering flame of a candle,
in the silence between the notes,
in the smell of the air.

The holy souls who carried the mortar,
who polished the floors,
who brought their babies for baptism,
and who mourned their loved ones at funerals.
The holy souls are here.

It is a cold place,
not unlike a mausoleum,
yet propelled into life though the …
    history
    wisdom
    perseverance

and faith
    that dwell here.
The coldness aches to be warmed
with love and friendship and devotion.

Can you hear their footsteps?
Can you imagine them lighting candles
a hundred years ago, just as you might today?
We smell the same incense,
we yearn for the same things,
and they remind us that we are connected across time,
and that when our warmth becomes cold we will live on,
not only through the structure of the church,
but not separate from it either.

Yes, the holy souls are here,
and we are here with them.

I wrote this while praying alone in St. Timothy's Episcopal Church in St. Louis County. The windows are indeed the most beautiful I have ever seen, but they are just windows, not the church. The community of its members is even more beautiful than the windows.

A New Church

I found a new church.
Its stained glass windows reflect new life,
fresh energy, diversity, abundance, and hope.
Deep greens and piercing blues,
stars and blood red,
bright light and yellows,
figures, both human and divine,
fellowship across time, place, and space,
connected in prayer and love,
in seeking and in trust and faith.

This is a church on the journey,
a church in progress,
striving to live the mission,
falling short on its own,
and thus led again to rely upon God.
Instead of trying to exercise authority,
energies channel toward exercising kindness,
gentleness, mutuality, and community.
Questions, and the people who bring them,
are welcomed in this new church.

It is a church alive today
because it is holy rooted in the past,
yet looking toward the future—
and its vision of the future is not one of clinging
to what no longer beckons life,
but of discovering what life longs for.
It is a struggle.
It is incomplete.
It is open, humble, discerning, and imperfect.

It is a church for today and tomorrow.
It is a church where Christ is no doubt present.
And perhaps it is a church that Magdalene, Peter,
James, Paul, and Chloe would find familiar.

Perspective

To see the earth as a whole
one must travel a long distance
to a place empty and cold,
isolated,
untethered,
dis-connected.
I wonder, can the astronaut feel
God's presence in the emptiness there?
Yet we sometimes try to get the big picture of God,
or really we pretend that we can see it,
that we have our arms around the Great Mystery,
but our arms are not long enough
and even if we could get that far from God
so as to see the whole
perhaps we would be so distant
as to be in hell,
a cold, lonely, sterile place
of thoughts, concepts, intellectual curiosity, and ego.
I don't want to read the catechism,
or even if I could,
to know what the libraries written about God say.

No, I want to be so very close to God
that I can taste and smell God's presence.
And I'm not even interested in comparing
the part I experience with the other parts,
whether I am being caressed by the hand,
or toenail, or strand of hair,
because when I am that close,
that is all that matters.

Notice the real (tiny) me hugging the sphere representing God in this painting, *Perspective*.
It is true that we can adopt a "both/and" rather than an "either/or" approach to experience
of God and knowledge about God, but I do have a preference.

I was so struck by the beautiful and majestic starkness of the sanctuary at Ladue Chapel Presbyterian Church, with a very tall ceiling, large clear windows, right angles, open—without pillars. All white, not just the walls but the pews as well. The only colors were found in the carpet and pew cushions (red), the small stained glass window over the altar, and a small vase of flowers.

Sanctuary

When God is not near the altar …
When there are no statues to remind or distract you …
When there is no water to bless you …
and when there are no people in this empty shell …
    It makes you look around …
        at your friends and the people you love
        at the people you fear
        at your life and how you spend your time
        and inside yourself
    It makes you look for where God really is.

All four Gospels include an account of the multiplication of the loaves and fishes, a lesson inviting us to share with compassion and generosity what we have. "And those who ate were about five thousand men, besides women and children." (Matthew 14:21)

5001

Five thousand men, plus women and children were fed.
Imagine the sense of amazement,
the sense of abundance,
the relaxing into companionship
that accompanies a shared experience,
especially when it involves food.
It truly was a miracle.
The pushing to be in a prime location
(close enough to hear Jesus well, on a patch
of grass, in front rather than behind the extra-large person)
faded away also.
Yes it was a shared experience of conviviality.
Unplanned, transitory yet memorable.
You could even say life-changing.

I wonder how those who arrived late were received,
the five thousand and first man, you might say.
Was he offered baskets of leftovers?
Did anyone move over to share a blanket on the ground?
Did anyone share the story of the miracle
that had just taken place?

And as we arrive early to stake our claim on a prime location
on Christmas Eve or Easter Sunday,
do we come with a sense of abundance?
Are we attentive to the twice-a-year churchgoers,
and if so, not wish they wouldn't try to squeeze in
but get up and offer our pew?
How surprised you both might be if you said,
"Pardon me, but this space is reserved … for you."

Living in the Present Moment

"And so I realized that, like making friends,
we can also make strangers,
and for a little while I forgot how to do that."

Surprise

If you live in today
you will welcome the surprise of tomorrow

Did You Notice?

Did you notice
God
standing over in the corner
or behind a tree
shy
naked
longing for your attention
hoping that you stop doing
whatever it is that preoccupies you,
keeps you from looking up
and squinting to find Her
—even if the busyness you are doing is for God—
gently, patiently, secretly hoping
you stop it
if only for a little while
to allow loving gazing at each other
holding hands
breathing each other's breath
and remembering
really remembering
why you exist.

Forever Friends

I want you to go to heaven,
I just don't want to go to your funeral.
Dear friend, you have taught me well …
about God,
about Love,
about faith,
about aging gracefully,
about true purpose in life,
about being present,
about friendship and companionship.
Do you really have to leave?
Will you find a way to remain in my heart?
Will you continue to love, encourage, and challenge me?
Will I find joy after the tears stop flowing?
Oh, won't you teach me the lesson about how to survive
the loss of a good friend?
Can you do this before you die
or is this how it must be taught?
I know you know, old friend.
And yet deep, deep in my heart
is the certainty that you will never leave me,
perhaps so deep that at times I may not be able to feel it.
So hug me now while we can.
Give me a mischievous wink,
a warm, welcoming smile,
a reassuring hand on the shoulder.
I love you dear friend, forever.

No Waiting

If I had to wait for those I will leave behind,
surely I could not be in heaven.
So when beaming up or over to that ephemeral place,
somehow all those I have loved,
all those who loved me,
and all those I dread leaving behind
will be there eager to greet me,
to welcome me into eternal love, eternal life.

Spirits don't age and they are easier to recognize
because of the transparency,
no hiding behind wrinkles, clothes, insecurity, or fear—
just authentic love,
naked spirit.
Oh, how I long to hug in the spiritual realm,
fusion, union as we now long for with God
and as God sometimes teases.

Loving God, let me remember that the deeper reality
is unitive,
is timeless,
is completely free and loving,
and let me live with that awareness here in this realm.
Let me help heaven break into earth just a little bit more.

On the Day I Die

Oh loving God, let the day I die be familiar.
Let me recall at least one dear memory.
Let me be present with at least one person who loves me.
Let me feel you with me, Sweet Jesus, my friend.
Let me surrender all to you,
as I have begged to do so many times before.
Let me live my last breath in the moment.
Let me rejoice in your love
and in the life that surrounds me.
Let me notice something beautiful that day.
And let my last words
(and my words every day until that day)
be "Thank you, my love, for everything."

Born Again

Let me be born again
like I have actually died
completely free
and knowing that the only
way to touch another
is through love

Flowers at My Funeral

I don't want flowers at my funeral.
Instead of giving flowers, give hugs.
I want my wake to be a celebration of the joy of life,
an acceptance that dying is a part of living.

I don't want photos posted of happy times over the decades,
but instead I want everyone to embrace the moment,
with laughter
and stories of love and adventure,
stories of seeking and surrender,
perhaps some momentary sobbing,
and occasional welling of tears,
but certainly an abundance of good food.
If there could be cooking at my wake
that would be great!
Maybe a barbecue and grilled veggies,
and chocolate desserts.

When we forget that our bodies are dying
are we fully aware of the gift of life?
Isn't death the threshold that most profoundly
reveals that love endures forever,
conquers all, and is the point of existence?

So don't try to be strong, but surrender to love,
and to the tears, pain, suffering, joy, and laughter love brings.
Surrender to love at my death, and always,
and there we will live forever.

*Shortly after raising his friend Lazarus from the dead, Jesus dined with
Lazarus and his two sisters, Mary and Martha. Anticipating Jesus'
death, Mary anointed Jesus' feet and wiped them with her hair.
(John 11 and 12:1-11)*

Resurrection

I want to feel like Lazarus,
free from what bound me,
refreshed and clean,
accepting Jesus' friendship
and the invitation to recline with him at table,
unafraid of death while knowing that it may come soon,
savoring the fragrance of pure love,
willing to live to the fullest in this moment,
and being inexpressibly grateful for that opportunity.

Anointing a terminally ill friend with perfumed oils. We sat on the sofa in her home, knowing that sometimes there is no "right" thing to do or say. Knowing that simply being present with one another is the best way to express love and friendship.

Foresight

Looking up,
lying in a casket,
what will I see?
Lord, let me see it now,
that I may be free
to live my last day
each day,
to welcome today
as my last opportunity
for reconciliation,
for my last kiss while in
this unresurrected body.
Let me speak the truth of my heart,
and let me say each good-bye
with a peaceful smile.

Heartbeat

If you wish to experience the heartbeat of God,
welcome the quiet,
welcome the present,
gently place your hand over your chest …
and listen.

Hungry

If your soul is hungry, feed it beauty.

Our Last Christmas

This could be our last Christmas together.
Whether we are painfully aware of it
because of the progression of Alzheimer's
or debilitation, the chemotherapy,
or the unspoken about separation growing between us,
or whether we are not so aware
that the car accident or burst aneurysm is but one heartbeat away,
this could be our last Christmas together.
So may we treasure this day.
So may we treasure each other.
May we let go of the sensitivity to annoyance,
the urge to judge, the need to be right,
and the compulsion to control.
May we let go, if only for a while, the hurts of the past
inflicted by those who loved us badly.
Let us mediate Christ's coming anew into the world
and the gifts of love, forgiveness, acceptance,
and freedom he offers.
This could be our last Christmas together.

A Place to Pray

Is there a better place to pray than here,
wherever "here" happens to be?
Aren't all places good places to pray?
And so is this one.
I am welcomed by water teeming with life …
flowering lilies, duckweed, minnows,
a rabbit (believing it is safely out of sight) nibbling clover,
ducks and sitting rocks,
a bird that I don't recognize, large and beautiful,
singing of other feathered friends.
The sounds of water falling,
insects,
leaves in the gentlest of breezes
under a sky decorated with clouds,
white, blue, grey.
Artists painting landscapes.
The smell of cigarette smoke from visiting lovers.

Is there a better place to say thank you for this day,
this time,
the ability to see, hear, smell, taste, and feel,
the luxury of leisure that allows me
to simply sit and be in this place?
Surely, just to notice is prayer in itself,
accepting the invitation of revelation.
Oh God, you love me so, so much,
much more than I deserve,
yet I think I hear you inviting me
to enter more fully into life and joy with you,
and to join with you in inviting others to do the same.

Christmas Every Day

Each time a child is born,
we are invited to believe that God is with us,
not in the far reaches of our concept of heaven,
but inseparably close as our own flesh,
bone, blood, thoughts, emotions, and desires.
God chooses to be with us and within us.
God chooses that each infant be born
as an expression of new life,
intense hope, and tangible love,
unconditional, tangible love.

Through each birth we are invited to believe
that in and through God we are already united,
and that in and through our humanness we are united
in the hope that new life brings …
the hope for something more,
the fleeting awareness that we exist on the frontier
of the expansion of the universe,
that our existence is the manifestation of love
and its desire to connect with others,
and its desire to grow,
and its desire for complete giving and receiving,
for union,
communion.

With each death we are invited to recognize
that union is once again fulfilled,
that the circle of love is completed once more,
that with new life come uncertainty and adventure
and perhaps some fear preceding deeper trust,
and in all of it,
God is still present.

With each awakening—metaphorical ones—but
also with each disruption of sleep,
we are invited to remember that love gave us life.
Each day we are invited to accept that
our purpose is to cooperate with love.

I painted this on December 24, imagining a poor, young woman giving birth alone at the end of an alley while shoppers hurried by, oblivious to her, her needs, or the miracle of new life. The ancient Christmas story continues today, as does our need for a savior.

An important part of the spiritual journey is surrendering our ego, yet is
there anything more egotistical than wanting to live forever, or even be
remembered forever for that matter? The Bible tells us the story of Adam
and Eve in the Garden of Eden, the serpent tempting Eve by saying,
"You will not die; for God knows that when you eat of it your eyes will
be opened, and you will be like God, knowing good and evil." (Genesis
3:4–5). And after eating the fruit, "… the LORD God said, 'See, the
man has become like one of us, knowing good and evil; and now, he
might reach out his hand and take also from the tree of life, and eat, and
live forever' – therefore the LORD God sent him forth from the garden
of Eden …" (Genesis 3:22–23).

My Biggest Secret

Do you wish to know something about me
that may surprise or perhaps shock you?
Do you wish to know a secret that may cause you to wonder,
or question what you thought was certain?

If today were the last day of my existence,
I would accept that.
If I am gifted with another day tomorrow,
I will accept that as well.
I have been so privileged and blessed,
more than enough, much more than most.
I am not striving to attain eternal life,
instead I share in it now,
because life is eternal.

I do not cower from the expectation
that I will completely melt into nothingness and wholeness.

For me, heaven is not then, but is now, today.
Heaven is not to be earned or even received.
For me—the one who will no longer exist,
perhaps as soon as tomorrow—
heaven exists in the eternal state of now.
For me, heaven is living in harmony
with the purpose for which I was created,
as best I can comprehend it.
Namely, to love, to be loved, to give love, to accept love.
That simple.
That true.

If I have been in love today,
I have been in heaven and within God,
and the lie that we should seek something else,
something illusory rather than real,
dulls our sense of fundamental purpose
and the urgency with which we are to embrace it.

We have still not learned the lesson of Eve and the serpent:
that it is not authentic for us to aspire to be like God,
all knowing and immortal.
And so we cast ourselves out of recognition
that we live in Eden.

Please don't keep this a secret,
but instead proclaim the truth by loving now.

Pierced

I was seven years old the first time it happened to me,
staring at some busy ants, my eyes lost focus
and out of "nowhere" suddenly,
the awareness,
out of my self,
knowing that this world, this existence,
is an act of discretion.
It did not have to be.
We did not have to be.
I did not have to be.
So out of the suspended awe,
the silent question emerges, "Why?"
and like holding my breath,
it only lasts a long moment.
No point in even trying to cling to
what I had no power to cause or control.
I had no answer to the simple question then.

Last night it returned, You returned
with your mind-tingling gift,
this existence did not have to exist.
So why, what is the point?
Being older, I can at least posit an answer,
but what became so very clear at that moment,
what pierced my soul in that moment of awareness
is that the only sensible behavior is kindness.
The only sensible behavior is kindness,
everywhere,
every time.

Familiar

At the grocery store
and even though I'd not been in a while,
most people looked familiar,
they looked human,
the beauty of being human peeked out from each person,
even if in a hurry, distracted, or focused,
even if grumpy,
I could see their beauty,
and I welcomed them …
    with acknowledgement,
    a glance,
    a smile,
    a "you go first"
    with an absence of fear and guardedness.
I was singing out loud in that store—
who knew shopping could be so joy-filled?
And so I realized that, like making friends,
we can also make strangers,
and for a little while I forgot how to do that.
I realized that my willingness to become vulnerable,
and welcome my authentic self,
was bearing fruit.

"Be still, and know that I am God!"
(Psalm 46:10)

46:10

Stop…
    Stop…
        Stop…
            and listen

Know that I am love
    Know that love is
        Know that existence is love
            that existence is of love

    Experience that existence is of love

Stop … and experience that existence is of love

Trust that this is enough
    Trust that this is my (God's) desire
    Let go
        Surrender to love
        Rest in love
            Abide in me
                As
                    I abide in you

Appendix: A Group Resource

Everyday Sacred is perfectly suited as a resource for small faith groups, groups on retreat, book clubs, and others who wish to journey together for a while in the hope of becoming more aware of God's presence in their daily lives and deepening their sense of community around that common desire. The following discussion outline offers suggested reflection questions for each of a series of eight gatherings, based on the book's introduction and seven chapters. With this outline, I invite you to notice and celebrate the sacredness that fills our lives and to share your experiences with others wishing to do the same.

Between the group's gatherings, each member is invited to use the contents of the upcoming chapter for daily prayer and reflection. You may find it helpful to use a journal to jot down how you have noticed God in your life, questions that arise within you, what happens during prayer, reflections of your own, or poems that God may give you. If you keep a journal, bring it to the group meetings to facilitate sharing.

First Gathering—Introduction
- What is your conversion story?
- As you enter into this group journey, what are you hoping for?
- How have you most often and/or most powerfully experienced God?
- What is your practice of prayer?
- Have you ever created art as a form of prayer or used art to inspire prayer?

Second Gathering—Nature
- Which meditation or painting inspired the strongest reaction within you, and what was that reaction?
- Are there meditations or paintings in this chapter that resonate with your own experience, and if so, which one(s)?
- Is there a particular aspect of nature that you find reveals God to you more powerfully than others: for example, the ocean, the sky, the earth, animals, or trees?
- Do you find it helpful to pray outdoors?

Third Gathering—Home
- Which meditation or painting inspired the strongest reaction within you, and what was that reaction?
- Are there meditations or paintings in this chapter that resonate with your own experience, and if so, which one(s)?
- Name three strong memories of your experience of home as a child. Is it apparent to you that God was present during those experiences, and if so, how?
- What are some of the defining characteristics of home for you today?
- Do you find it helpful to pray at home, and if so, do you have a special prayer place (for example, a comfortable chair, a candle, or an icon)?

Fourth Gathering—Family

- Which meditation or painting inspired the strongest reaction within you, and what was that reaction?
- Are there meditations or paintings in this chapter that resonate with your own experience, and if so, which one(s)?
- Reflect upon your relationships with members of your immediate family, and also your extended family. How is God present (or what is God inviting you to) in those relationships?
- Does your family experience God *as a family*, and if so, how?
- Do members of your family experience God in ways different from you?

Fifth Gathering—Jesus

- Which meditation or painting inspired the strongest reaction within you, and what was that reaction?
- Jesus asked his disciples, "But who do you say that I am?" (Luke 9:20) How do *you* answer that question?
- Who does Jesus say you are?
- What is your reaction to considering the humanness of Jesus that is depicted in some of the meditations?
- What do you wish to say to Jesus now?

Sixth Gathering—Holy Communion

- Which meditation or painting inspired the strongest reaction within you, and what was that reaction?
- Are there meditations or paintings in this chapter that resonate with your own experience, and if so, which one(s)?

- Have you had any particularly powerful experiences while sharing in the Lord's Supper, and if so, what were they?

Seventh Gathering—Church

- Which meditation or painting inspired the strongest reaction within you, and what was that reaction?
- Are there meditations or paintings in this chapter that resonate with your own experience, and if so, which one(s)?
- What, if anything, do you wish for from church (or another sacred community if you do not consider yourself a member of a church)?
- What, if anything, do you welcome the church to expect from you?

Eighth Gathering—Living in the Present Moment

- Which meditation or painting inspired the strongest reaction within you, and what was that reaction?
- Are there meditations or paintings in this chapter that resonate with your own experience, and if so, which one(s)?
- What, if any, have been your experiences with death, and how was God present in those experiences?
- Are there certain practices that you use to help you live more fully in the present moment?
- As these gatherings come to a close, do you have a sense of how God feels about you right now, and what God wishes to say to you?

Some of the images in this book
may be purchased as note cards
by visiting www.clarenceheller.com.

Clarence J. Heller is a spiritual director, poet, and dreamer whose writing and paintings are inspired through prayerful reflection. Early in his career he worked as an engineer, later completed his MBA, and then received a second masters from Aquinas Institute of Theology. Currently his work focuses on leading guided prayer retreats situated in everyday life. Clarence is the proud father of two adult children, and he lives in St. Louis, Missouri with his wife and their beloved dog, Maya.